S0-AVT-489

THE PUSHKIN MUSEUM
OF FINE ARTS, MOSCOW

THE PUSHKIN MUSEUM OF FINE ARTS, MOSCOW

PAINTING

Aurora Art Publishers · Leningrad

Compiled and introduced by Irina Antonova
Translated from the Russian by Elena Bessmertnaya
Designed by Leonid Zykov

© Aurora Art Publishers, Leningrad, 1983, 1988
PRINTED AND BOUND IN THE USSR

$Г \dfrac{4903020000\text{-}615}{023(01)\text{-}88}$ КБ-50-30-86

ISBN 5-7300-0106-1

The Pushkin Museum of Fine Arts is one of the major art museums in the Soviet Union. It houses a wealth of works of world art dating from earliest times to the present day. Nowadays the Museum's diverse and comprehensive collections number more than half a million items.

Pride of place undoubtedly goes to the Museum's picture gallery, which enjoys world-wide renown. Among its treasures are Byzantine icons, works by Botticelli, Cranach, Rembrandt, Poussin, Rubens, Watteau, Tiepolo, Monet, Renoir, Cézanne, Matisse, Picasso, as well as masterpieces by many other European artists of the fifteenth to twentieth centuries.

The history of the Museum goes back to the 1750s. It was then that the idea of establishing in Moscow a museum of fine arts to display the relics of classical antiquity was first voiced. Among its ardent supporters were professors of Moscow University. In 1894, Professor Ivan Tsvetayev, who headed the department of art history at Moscow University, in his speech at the first congress of Russian artists appealed to the public to make donations for the construction of the building that was to house the Museum. Four years later a committee for the foundation of the Museum was set up, with Moscow's outstanding scholars, artists and sculptors among its members.

Tsvetayev managed to win the financial support of the city's business-men, and finally, though with difficulty, the sum sufficient for the construction of the Museum was raised. The foundation-stone of the Museum was laid in 1898. Fourteen years later, on May 31, 1912 (June 13 N. S.), the Museum of Fine Arts was inaugurated. The building was designed by the Moscow architect Roman Klein. It assumed a noticeable place in Moscow's architectural ensemble, and today it is still one of the city's major public buildings.

Tsvetayev conceived the Museum of Fine Arts mainly as an educational institution to be closely linked with Moscow University. The basic collection consisted of copies of the famous sculptural relics of Antiquity, the Middle Ages and the Renaissance. Tsvetayev personally took an active part in the formation of the collection: he ordered plaster casts from the finest statues displayed in the famous museums of Berlin, Munich, Paris, London, Rome and Naples to be made and brought to Moscow.

The October Revolution of 1917 was a turning point in the Museum's history. Grand projects were advanced for essential restructuring of the work of all the museums in the country. On March 27, 1924, the People's Commissariat for Public Education adopted a decree on reorganizing the Museum of Fine Arts and replenishing its collections with genuine works of art, first and foremost with paintings. The first two rooms of the picture gallery were inaugurated on November 10, 1924, at the time of the celebration of the seventh anniversary of the October Revolution. Simultaneously, an exhibition of the paintings which the Museum had received from the Hermitage and other Leningrad collections was held.

This was an event of truly momentous importance for the cultural life of Moscow at that time. To all intents and purposes, it gave the Museum of Fine Arts a new lease of life, since it was to become a museum containing genuine works of art. Its collections were set up in a way that had no precedent in the history of museums, namely through the selection and transference to it of works of art from other public museums and numerous private collections; in other words, through the redistribution of the country's national art treasures. This principle, implemented in the early post-revolutionary years, was based on considerations of national expedience. It was dictated not by reasons of taste, prestige or commercial utility, but by lofty revolutionary ideals: by the desire to make cultural treasures available to the masses. Lenin's decrees on the registration and preservation of works of art and the nationalization of art treasures, adopted in the first months after the Revolution, were of tremendous importance for the country's museums. The Decree of the Council of People's Commissars "On Banning the Removal of Objects of Art and Antiquity to Other Countries" (September 19, 1918) was actuated by an attempt to take abroad a painting of the Botticelli school *Madonna and Child*, which had been in the collection of Princess Yekaterina Meshcherskaya; today it is displayed at the Pushkin Museum of Fine Arts.

The period from 1924 to 1930 saw a rapid increase of the Museum's collection. It was then that a vast-scale organizational and research work was carried out, which consisted in the examination of hundreds of collections and thousands of works of art in order to select the most valuable of them for the Museum. This work was headed by prominent Soviet experts in Western European art: Nikolai Romanov, director of the Museum from 1923, who worked out a plan for its reorganization; Abram Efros, who was in charge of the department of French painting; and Victor Lazarev, an outstanding authority on Italian art. It is due to the competence and erudition of these men, their energy and enthusiasm, that the Museum now possesses impressive collections, first and foremost that of the Old Masters.

During those six years the Museum came to possess a rich collection of original works, some of which were real masterpieces. The main sources for amassing the collection were the Department of Fine Arts of the Rumiantsev Museum (which had been closed down by that time), the Tretyakov Gallery, which transferred to the Museum its collection of Western European art, and the Hermitage in Leningrad. A large number of pictures and other works of art came from nationalized private collections.

The year 1930 marked the end of the initial period of assembling the collection of paintings, when large private collections or parts of them were acquired. From the 1930s on, replenishment went along new lines, primarily by chance acquisitions from antique shops or from private collections. Also, novel opportunities for enriching the collection arose: purchases at temporary exhibitions, donations by collectors and artists and exchanges with other museums. Simultaneously, important work was done at the Museum to systematize and attribute the items acquired. In 1936 the Central Purchasing Commission (now the State Commission of Experts) was set up, charged with the task of buying works of art for museums as recommended by their boards of experts.

The active work carried out by the staff of the Museum of Fine Arts (which since 1937 has borne the name of the great Russian poet Pushkin) and aimed at further enlarging, studying and popularizing its collections, was interrupted by the war against Nazi Germany. Over 100,000 exhibits — paintings, sculptures, drawings, engravings, rare books, together with the Museum's archives — were evacuated to Siberia. The Museum staff members, both those who had remained in Moscow and those who had been evacuated, did their utmost to preserve every item intact. As the war began to draw to its close in 1944, the evacuated collection was brought back to Moscow. The roofings of the Museum building, damaged by the bombings, were repaired. Immediately work was started on arranging new displays; research and replenishment activities were resumed on a full scale. Of particular importance during this rehabilitation period was the work of the Museum's restorers headed by the well-known Soviet artist Pavel Korin. On October 3, 1946, the Museum was reopened to the public.

At the end of the war the Museum received for temporary keeping the art treasures of the Dresden Picture Gallery saved by the Soviet Army. The celebrated paintings discovered in the last weeks of the war in damp shelters in the environs of Dresden needed expert care. The Museum's staff carried out a vast amount of work registering the treasures and restoring some of them. In 1955 the priceless collections were handed over to the German Democratic Republic in order to strengthen and further develop friendly relations between the peoples of the two countries. The year 1948 was also important for the Museum, since it was decided to distribute the collections of the Moscow Museum of Modern Western Art between the Hermitage in Leningrad and the Pushkin Museum of Fine Arts. The Museum of Modern Western Art had comprised the collections of two famous Moscow art collectors of the early twentieth century, Sergei Shchukin and Ivan Morozov. Nationalized in 1918, both collections existed as separate museums until 1923: the First (the Shchukin collection) and the Second (the Morozov collection) Museums of Modern Western Painting. In 1923 they formally merged into the Museum of Modern Western Art, which in 1925 became a branch of the Museum of Fine Arts. In 1928 both sections were brought together under the same roof (in the building which had formerly housed the Morozov collection), and the Museum of Modern Western Art became a museum in its own right.

From the first years of the existence of the Museum of Modern Western Art, its staff undertook an energetic campaign to enrich its collection, concentrating mainly on contemporary revolutionary art. Due to purchases at exhibitions and artists' donations, the Museum of Modern Western Art doubled its collection in a comparatively short time.

The transference of pictures from the Museum of Modern Western Art to the Museum of Fine Arts was a particularly significant contribution: now its collections covered a much longer period and included works by modern artists.

Exchanges of works of art between Soviet museums and those in the socialist countries have recently become a new way of enlarging collections. Paintings, graphic works and sculptures have been received from the German Democratic Republic, Bulgaria and Czechoslovakia.

The Museum continues its regular purchases of works of art through the mediation of the State Commission of Experts. Purchases of works of art abroad and at the art exhibitions held in Moscow by foreign countries have assumed a larger scale. Periodically, the Museum arranges special exhibitions of newly acquired items. In 1985 there was founded a special Museum of Private Collections Donated to the State, which is functioning as the Pushkin Museum's department.

The collections of the Pushkin Museum of Fine Arts have been formed during more than seventy five years. They give a good idea of the development of world art, of the main stages of this development and of various national artistic schools and their major exponents.

The picture gallery's display begins with a group of Byzantine icons, among which there are several rare pieces. The fourteenth-century icon of *St. Pantaleon* painted in tempera is a classical sacred image, characterized by flat frontal position of the representation. The icons of *The Twelve Apostles, The Annunciation* and *The Dormition* by masters of the Constantinople school are among the finest creations of Byzantine art in the first half of the fourteenth century. During that period Byzantine icon painting partly lost its inherent monumental quality, but it acquired some secular elements and regained the features of late classical antiquity. The author of *The Twelve Apostles* succeeded in creating a free, unconstrained composition; all the figures are dynamic and seem to be united by a common spirit. The icon is imbued with an air of manly force and intense concentration.

The early stage in the evolution of Western European painting is illustrated by a small but impressive collection of works by thirteenth- and fourteenth-century Italian artists. Two thirteenth-century icons hold a central place in this collection: *Madonna and Child Enthroned* by an anonymous Pisan artist and a large altarpiece of the Florentine school, which also shows the enthroned Madonna and Child with scenes from her life. The former icon, with its exquisite interplay of golden lines and its image of the Madonna, at once spiritual and permeated with deep human feeling, shows an obvious influence of Byzantine art. The latter work, on the contrary, anticipates the features that eventually came to dominate the Florentine school of painting: the energetic plastic modelling of the figures and the use of local colours.

The fifteenth century — the age of the early Italian Renaissance — is represented in the Museum mainly by the works of artists who still retained Late Gothic traditions in their work. Their pictures testify to the complex evolution of Renaissance art and its transitional character, to the rivalry of various trends in painting, to the diversity of local schools of painting and the individuality of the artists' styles. This group includes the polyptych *Madonna and Child with Saints* by Francesco d'Antonio de Ancona, *The Beheading of John the Baptist* by Sano di Pietro, and two panels representing the images of saints by Sassetta. The latter is known as the greatest Quattrocento artist of Siena. Like all the Sienese, he possessed a subtle feeling for line. His figures captivate the viewer by their fragile grace and delicately elongated proportions.

The characteristic Renaissance features of Italian painting, which rejected medieval asceticism and made Man and Nature the focal point of interest, are exemplified by the works of artists active in the late fifteenth and early sixteenth centuries. *Madonna and Child* by Perugino, the teacher of Raphael, is an incarnation of serene calm and spiritual balance, of the joy and devotion of motherhood. Sandro Botticelli's *Annunciation*, one of the Museum's masterpieces, was painted in the later dramatic period of the artist's life. Despite the inner turmoil of the characters, the painting is evocative of exalted emotions and conveys Botticelli's adoration of the beauty of man.

The Museum possesses a comparatively large collection of sixteenth-century paintings, both by artists who followed the traditions of the High Renaissance masters, and those who chose to take their own path in art. The former include a large group of Leonardo's followers and disciples. The artists of the Venetian school, too, figure prominently in the Museum's picture gallery. Paolo Veronese, a master of gorgeous pageantry, is represented by several works, of which the finest are *Minerva*, a small sketch for a mural, and the painting *The Rest on the Flight into Egypt*, executed in the artist's later period. There are also several works by the painters of Northern Italy.

In the fifteenth and sixteenth centuries the Netherlandish school came to the fore in North European painting. The Museum's earliest Netherlandish pieces date back to the late fifteenth century and the first decades of the sixteenth century. They give a good idea of their authors' diverse creative searches and the coexistence of varied trends and traditions in Netherlandish painting: the Late Gothic traditions, the Italianate trend and the new realistic trends.

The worthiest works, however, show the Netherlandish artists' endeavour for direct observation, for rendition of space, and depiction of the characteristic, inimitable traits of every phenomenon, person or thing. Jan Mostaert's *Ecce Homo* is notable for the strikingly expressive faces of the Gospel personages. Herri met de Bles in his *Road to Calvary* pays much more attention to the mountainous landscape than to the characters that ought to be the focal point of the composition. *The Adoration of the Magi* and *The Nativity* by two anonymous artists of the first half of the sixteenth century have in common their authors' striving to turn the Gospel subjects into festive, almost theatrical scenes.

The collection of fifteenth- and sixteenth-century German paintings comprises several excellent pieces that illustrate the basic features of the art of Germany, where the Renaissance began to develop fifty years later than in Italy. In fifteenth-century German painting medieval forms still dominate, though the treatment of religious subjects definitely leans towards the narrative and there is a profusion of details from daily life. The Museum's earliest German paintings are two panels of the Sebenstein altarpiece (*The Nativity* and *The Adoration of the Magi*) by the Master of the Liechtenstein Castle. Both compositions are permeated with an air of utmost piety. They still retain features which were characteristic of Gothic art: the absence of clear space representation, weightlessness of figures and abundance of gold.

The early decades of the sixteenth century were the heyday of the German Renaissance. The dramatic *Crucifixion* by the Swabian Master of Messkirch and the panel of an altarpiece *The Flight into Egypt* by a monogrammist AB belong to this period; some parts of the altarpiece are in the Dresden Picture Gallery. There are some remarkable works by Lucas Cranach the Elder, one of the greatest painters of the German Renaissance. His *Virgin and Child* conveys lyricism and serenity. Cranach managed to show harmony between man and the world around him. He was one of the first to depict his native land — the mountainous regions of Southern Germany. *The Effects of Jealousy (The Silver Age)* bears witness to the humanistic predisposition of Cranach, who took his subject from Hesiod's poem *Works and Days.* Cranach's influence is easily traceable in *The Allegory of Love* by the Swabian painter Matthias Gerung — a fine specimen of a picture intended for connoisseurs. Gerung illustrates the all-conquering power of love with three subjects from classical mythology and the Bible.

The collection of seventeenth-century paintings by Dutch, Flemish, French, Italian and Spanish artists is one of the largest in the picture gallery. It includes works by Rembrandt, Jacob van Ruisdael, Nicolas Poussin, Claude Lorrain, Peter Paul Rubens, Jacob Jordaens, Francisco de Zurbarán, Bartolomé Esteban Murillo, Bernardo Strozzi and Domenico Fetti. Dutch painting is probably most amply represented. While in the works of the early seventeenth-century painters Abraham Bloemaert and Hendrick Goltzius the Italianate traditions are still appreciable and the pictures of the Utrecht artist Gerard van Honthorst strongly manifest the influence of Caravaggio, the unassuming portraits by Jan Ravesteyn and Paulus Moreelse, the genre scenes by Dirk Hals and Pieter Codde, and Hendrick Avercamp's landscape *Winter Scene with Skaters* signify the beginning of the Dutch national school. These artists worked in diverse genres striving for a truthful depiction of everyday life. The Dutch landscapists are represented by several superb pieces. Notable for their poetic works with an emphasis on light-and-air effects are two artists of the first half of the seventeenth century — Jan van Goyen (*View of the Waal at Nijmegen, Hay-making*) and Salomon van Ruysdael (*River Landscape, River Crossing*). *View of Egmond aan Zee* by Jacob van Ruisdael, undoubtedly the greatest master among the Dutch realist landscape painters, stands out for its broad generalizations and deep dramatic power of feeling.

Scenes of everyday life, a genre which flourished in Holland in the 1640s—1660s, were created by some very famous painters. Those by Adriaen van Ostade (*A Scene in the Inn, Drunken Brawl, A Peasant Feast*) are sharply grotesque. The picture gallery possesses Ostade's striking *Flute Player*, showing a pathetic, lonely figure, painted with rare sincerity and warm sympathy. The works of Gabriel Metsu (*Girl Doing Needlework, A Duet*), executed with remarkable exquisiteness and meticulous care for detail, are profoundly humane and truthful. Gerard Ter Borch ranks among the most sensitive painters of the seventeenth century. His *Portrait of a Lady* is remarkable for the noble artistry of design and the poetic effect of grey tones. The two canvases by Pieter de Hooch (*Morning of a Young Man* and *A Sick Child*) characterize the early and the late periods of his work respectively. They are imbued with that special air of intimacy, which is characteristic of de Hooch's finest works. There are some outstanding paintings by Emanuel de Witte (*Market in the Port, A Church Interior*), who succeeded in lending a new scope to the traditionally small forms of Dutch scenes of everyday life: de Witte placed his characters in a bustle of market-places or in spacious church interiors. The collection of Dutch still lifes makes it possible to trace the development of this genre through all its stages, beginning with the works of its founders — the Haarlem painters Pieter Claesz. and Willem Claesz. Heda.

There is no doubt that pride of place goes to the Museum's six Rembrandts. Rembrandt van Rijn was able to convey with unprecedented profoundness and force the world of human emotions and the inner beauty of man. *Christ Driving the Money-changers from the Temple* (1626) is a major work dating from Rembrandt's early period. *The Incredulity of St. Thomas* reflects the author's creative searches in the first half of the 1630s. His *Portrait of an Old Woman, Portrait of an Elderly Woman* and *Portrait of Adriaen van Rijn* (?), painted in the mid-1650s, are among Rembrandt's best. They are included in a group of portraits which art critics have called life-story portraits. *Ahasuerus, Haman and Esther* (1660) is a recognized masterpiece, in which the artist was able to reveal the innermost feelings of his characters. The dramatic conflict of the people depicted is reflected in the blend of red and golden tones, suffused with shining light; the hues of light and colour seem to be the equivalents of spiritual and ethical values.

It was not until 1961, when an exhibition of the Museum's seventeenth- and eighteenth-century Italian painting was held, that the large and impressive collection of seventeenth-century Italian paintings was fully appreciated. Since that time regular studies of this collection have been conducted, for there are still a number of pictures which need more precise attribution. It is worth noting that here the works with realistic and romantic features outnumber those bearing the stamp of official court art.

An important contribution to the development of the realist trend in Italian painting in the first half of the seventeenth century was made by artists who worked in Venice. The best-known pieces are those by Domenico Fetti (*David with the Head of Goliath*), Johann Liss (*The Punishment of Marsyas*), Bernardo Strozzi (*An Old Coquette, Feeding of the Five Thousand, An Astronomer and His Disciple*).

The collection of seventeenth-century French painting, too, boasts a few masterpieces. The two rival trends at the beginning of the century are represented by Simon Vouet's large-scale *Annunciation* (an example of court style) and by Valentin's *The Denial of St. Peter*, which bears an unmistakable imprint of Caravaggio's democratic ideas. The focus of attention here is undoubtedly the works of Nicolas Poussin and Claude Gellée (Lorrain), which give an ample idea of Classicism, the dominant trend in the art of the period. The Museum's Poussins date from different periods of the artist's creative career. *The Victory of Joshua over the Amorites* illustrates the artist's early period; *Rinaldo and Armida*, one of the Museum's masterpieces, demonstrates Poussin's strongest points: the rendering of noble feelings of his personages and the superb harmony of colour and composition. *The Magnanimity of Scipio*, a work of mature Classicism, appears to be somewhat didactic while *Landscape with Hercules and Cacus* is among the finest achievements of Poussin's later years.

Nature was always accorded a prominent place by the exponents of French Classicism. The highest achievements in the landscape genre are Claude Lorrain's *Morning*, *Evening* and, especially, *The Rape of Europa*. These pieces, permeated with a poetic mood, were inspired both by the traditions of Greek and Roman art and by vivid impressions of Italian scenery. Lorrain's landscapes are filled with light and air, they are serene and beautifully balanced.

The collection of seventeenth-century Flemish paintings includes the works of such celebrated artists as Peter Paul Rubens, Jacob Jordaens, Frans Snyders and Anthony van Dyck. The six Rubenses represent the vigorous art of the greatest Fleming, who glorified the joy of life and the sensual beauty of man. Rubens' *Bacchanalia* is a fine picture of mythological subject. It is a true paean to the bounty of nature. The artist's splendid achievements in portrait painting are illustrated by his female portrait. *The Apotheosis of Duchess Isabella*, *The Last Supper* and *Gaius Mucius Scaevola* impress the viewers by the beautiful brushwork, dynamic compositional arrangement and powerful imagery. The best of the Museum's three portraits by Van Dyck, *Portrait of Jan van den Wouwer*, shows Van Dyck, Rubens' favourite pupil, as a subtle and sophisticated portraitist. The works of Jacob Jordaens (*A Satyr Visiting a Peasant, Ulysses in the*

Cavern of Polyphemus, The Flight into Egypt) reveal the specific features of Flemish genre painting showing its concern with the everyday aspect of contemporary life. The major name in Flemish still-life painting is that of Frans Snyders (*Still Life with a Swan, The Fish Shop*). This genre is also represented by the works of Jan Fyt and Daniel Seghers. The pictures of Adriaen Brouwer (*A Scribe, The Fight*), who excelled in depicting scenes of peasant life, are notable for their author's striking painterly skill. Flemish landscape painting is exemplified by works of Jan Siberechts (*The Ford*) and Jan Brueghel the Elder (Velvet Brueghel), who was Rubens' friend.

The small collection of seventeenth-century Spanish paintings comprises works of all the greatest artists of the period but Veláz-quez. These paintings give an idea of the characteristic features of the Spanish realist artists: their excellent feeling for nature, austere imagery and predominance of religious subjects. *The Virgin and Child* by Francisco de Zurbarán of Seville is an unpretentious, yet sublime study of motherly love. The few objects placed on the table are quite important, inasmuch as the author, in his inimitable laconic manner, uses them to reveal the simple life of common people. A pre-dilection for the depiction of popular life is typical of Bartolomé Esteban Murillo, who created a number of genre scenes featuring children — the young inhabitants of the streets of Seville (*Girl Selling Fruit*). Antonio de Pereda, a well-known painter of religious subjects, is also famous for his still lifes. His *Still Life with a Clock* is a variation of the Spanish artists' favourite motif: a group of vessels differing in form and colour.

French painting of the turn of the eighteenth century is repre-sented by a group of ceremonial portraits, of which the finest is the *Portrait of a Young Lady* by Nicolas de Largillière. The Museum's two pieces by the famous eighteenth-century artist Antoine Watteau, *The Bivouac* and *Satire on Physicians*, though dating from his early

18

period, are notable for the accuracy of details, sharply ironic presentation of characters, mixture of the illusory and the real, and last but not least, for the exquisite brushwork; these are the features typical of Watteau's mature works. The Museum also possesses several works by Watteau's followers: *Portrait of a Lady in the Garden* and *A Company at the Edge of a Wood* by Nicolas Lancret, and *Pastoral Scene* by Antoine Quillard. Jean-Baptiste Pater, Watteau's only pupil, is represented by *The Maypole Festival*. The Museum can offer viewers a splendid collection of works by François Boucher, which gives a comprehensive idea of this illustrious exponent of the Rococo style. In his charming *Jupiter and Callisto* Boucher treats the subject from classical mythology in a graceful and playful manner.

Eighteenth-century French art is characterized by the development of various genres of painting and the growth of democratic trends. This tendency is exemplified by two still lifes of Jean-Baptiste Siméon Chardin, the pictures of Jean-Baptiste Greuze (*The First Furrow*) and Jean-Honoré Fragonard (*A Poor Family*, *At the Fireside*), the portrait of Louis XVI executed by Joseph Siffred Duplessis and *The Leroy Family* by Nicolas-Bernard Lépicié.

The second half of the eighteenth century saw the flourishing of the landscapists Claude Joseph Vernet (*View of the Park of Villa Pamphili*) and Hubert Robert. Notable among the latter's many paintings is a small canvas *The Destruction of a Church*.

The works of Jacques Louis David displayed in the Museum were all painted in the eighteenth century. A study for *Andromache Mourning over Hector* of classical subject shows that David, the head of the school of Classicism in France, often drew inspiration from the glorious past. Two portraits painted in quite opposite styles (*Self-portrait* and *Portrait of a Young Man*) recommend David as a profound and truthful portrait painter, for whom the ideal man was one possessing natural simplicity and noble dignity.

The collection of eighteenth-century Italian paintings boasts several masterpieces, among which are works by Alessandro Magnasco of Genoa and Giuseppe Maria Crespi of Bologna, artists of the late seventeenth and early eighteenth centuries. *The Holy Family* and *Nymphs Disarming Cupids* by Crespi evince both the dramatic features of his painting and his inherent poetic and lyrical gift. *Clown Training a Magpie*, *The Crucifixion* and *Landscape with a Hermit* are all brilliant examples of Magnasco's expressive style.

The most outstanding achievements of eighteenth-century Italian painting are closely associated with Venice. The Museum has three works by the greatest Venetian Giovanni Battista Tiepolo: his early altarpiece *Madonna and Child with Saints* and two sketches in oil — *Two Saints* and *The Death of Dido*. The latter, a fine display of Tiepolo's consummate decorative skill and feeling for colour, captures the viewer by the superb conveyance of space, the unrestrained foreshortenings, dynamic movement and the spectacular richness of colour hues. Works by Giovanni Domenico Tiepolo (son of Giovanni Battista), Francesco Zugno, Sebastiano Ricci and Giovanni Battista Pittoni complete our notion of Venetian painting of that period.

There is also a valuable collection of works by Venetian landscapists, particularly of those who specialized in painting *vedutas*. The latter include Antonio Canaletto's *The Betrothal of the Venetian Doge to the Adriatic Sea* and a series of works by Bernardo Bellotto, dating from different periods of his life. The most valued items in this collection are *A Courtyard in Venice* and *A View in Venice* by Francesco Guardi, which are superb examples of eighteenth-century landscape painting. In his townscapes Guardi did not aim to depict views with much minuteness of detail, but he tried to convey the peculiar atmosphere of Venice, its inimitably picturesque, colourful and ever-changing appearance. He was able to capture, like no one before him, Venice's festive yet elegiac beauty. Displayed also is

Guardi's painting of a rare subject — *Alexander the Great Before the Corpse of Darius.*

Like most other European museums, the Pushkin Museum of Fine Arts possesses few works by English artists. The art of English portraiture is represented by the pictures of George Romney, John Hoppner, John Opie, Thomas Lawrence and George Dawe. The unique charm of the English landscape is conveyed by George Morland, Joseph Wright and John Crome. The gem of the collection is John Constable's *View of Highgate from Hampstead Heath.* Though a small study, it is evocative of the finest features of this illustrious English artist: the accuracy of observation, the freshness and ingenuousness of vision, the ability to produce a generalized poetic image of nature.

As to the nineteenth-century collection of European paintings, it certainly does not lack first-rate works. Precedence here is taken by the French school, though works of the early nineteenth century are not numerous, which is the case with most museums outside France. Prominent among the works of Jacques Louis David's pupils and followers are *Portrait of Napoleon* by François Gerard and *Equestrian Portrait of Prince Boris Yusupov* by Antoine Jean Gros. The pictures of religious subjects by Pierre Paul Prud'hon and Jean Auguste Dominique Ingres (*The Virgin Adoring the Eucharist*) bear the impact of the traditions of Classicism.

The Romantic movement, which dominated French painting in the early nineteenth century, is represented by two works of its major exponents, Eugène Delacroix and Théodore Géricault. The theme of shipwreck is one of Delacroix's favourite subjects (*After the Shipwreck*). He saw it as a poetic metaphor of man's life. Romantic painters tended to create dynamic compositions, using sharp light-and-shade contrasts and emotionally tense colours. *Study of a Male Model* is the only work by Théodore Géricault to be found in the museums of the Soviet Union. Géricault represents his model as a hero who challenges his millieu.

The collection of landscapes by French painters of the 1830s—1870s includes illustrious works by the artists of the Barbizon school: Théodore Rousseau, the founder of the school (*Cows at a Watering-place, In the Fontainebleau Woods*), Jules Dupré (*Evening, Ebbtide in Normandy, Oaks by the Road*), Constant Troyon (*The Approaching Thunderstorm*). Narcisse Diaz de la Peña (*A Rainy Day*) and Charles François Daubigny (*Morning, London, Evening in Honfleur*). These artists aimed at an exact and unprettified rendering of native scenery, painted on the spot.

The Museum possesses a superb collection of works by Jean-Baptiste Camille Corot, one of the most poetic and inspired landscapists of the nineteenth century. Among the finest pieces are both his early works (*Morning in Venice*) and those executed in his mature period (*Gust of Wind, Haycart, Stormy Weather. The Shore of Pas-de-Calais*). Corot's painting is characterized by tonal values independent of local colour. He avoided bright hues in favour of the silver-greys and golden-browns. His exceptional sensitivity of vision made him a precursor of the Impressionists.

Gustave Courbet is represented in the Museum only by landscapes, of which the finest, *A Hut in the Mountains*, belongs to his later, Swiss period. The landscape is executed with the vigour typical of Courbet, who created a generalized and majestic image of nature. Jean-François Millet's *Brushwood Gleaners* shows the artist's usual subject — his native scenery and peasant labour.

The collection of French Impressionists and Post-Impressionists at the Pushkin Museum of Fine Arts enjoys world-wide fame. Every major artist of the movement is amply represented, with one unfortunate exception: the Museum has only two works by Édouard Manet, *In the Bar ("Le Bouchon")* and *Portrait of Antonin Proust*, both unfinished. Claude Monet, the leading member of the Impressionist group, is presented with remarkable fullness, from his early *Luncheon on the Grass* to the works executed in the 1910s, in which the decorative trend predominates. The finest Monets (*Le Boulevard des Capucines in Paris, Seagulls, Rouen Cathedral at Noon*), the landscapes of Camille Pissarro (*Avenue de l'Opéra in Paris, Ploughland*) and Alfred Sisley (*Frosty Morning in Louveciennes*) charm with their amazing freshness, airiness, keen feeling for nature and poetic visual sensation. The Impressionists endeavoured to catch the fleeting, spontaneous impressions of the life around them, to render its rhythms and motions. They introduced pure colours and very characteristic brushwork — light, small, bright dabs of complementary colour, fusing in the eye of the spectator at a distance.

The Museum's five Renoirs are all superb pieces. One can hardly find a more perfect nude painting by Pierre Auguste Renoir than the one displayed at the Museum or a portrait more fascinating than his *Portrait of the Actress Jeanne Samary*. Renoir's art is imbued with the joy of life and admiration for the beautiful. The artist is captivated by his models' feminine charm, and he conveys his feelings by means of colour, revelling in a profusion of subtle shades of radiant colours saturated with light.

Edgar Degas' pictures of dancers and horse-races show him as a keen and meticulous observer, who excelled in depicting expressive motions and gestures of his characters. At least three of the Museum's fourteen Cézannes — *The Banks of the Marne, Still Life with Peaches and Pears* and *Pierrot and Harlequin (Mardi Gras)* — are among the best works of this great French artist of the late nineteenth and early twentieth century. In these pieces, Paul Cézanne brought his composition and colour scheme to the perfection which he endeavoured to achieve throughout all his life. Like the Impressionists, Cézanne strove to renew art, but he wanted to attain this by revealing the most general and permanent properties of objects — volume, structure and solidity. For him, colour was the only means of modelling.

The complex and contradictory inner world of Vincent van Gogh manifests itself with tremendous artistic vigour in *The Convict Prison* and in the bright, sun-drenched *Landscape at Auvers After the Rain*. Van Gogh's tormented sensibility is reflected in his images of enormous emotional vitality and spiritual sublimity. These images bear witness to Van Gogh's boundless love of man and to his search for justice.

The Museum's collection of paintings by Paul Gauguin is one of the largest in the world. Worthy of note among the works of his French period are *Café at Arles* and *Still Life with Fruit*. Outstanding among the Tahitian works, which are marked by an air of solemn tranquillity, are *The King's Wife, Are You Jealous?* and *Gathering Fruit*. There on Tahiti Gauguin sought harmony, happiness and freedom among simple and strong people unspoiled by bourgeois civilization. Leaning towards monumental and schematized forms, Gauguin used large areas of local colour which appeared to be suffused with sunlight.

The other nineteenth-century European schools of painting — though modest, as compared with the French school in the number of exhibits and their artistic value — nevertheless illustrate with sufficient clarity the development of democratic and realistic trends in nineteenth-century European art. The most comprehensive is the collection of German painting of the period, starting with the works of the most distinguished exponent of the German Romantic movement Caspar David Friedrich (*Mountain Landscape*). Arnold Böcklin's work (*Spring*) is also evocative of Romantic traditions.

In the collection of twentieth-century European painting, precedence is again assumed by French artists. The Museum's blue and pink Picassos are famous throughout the world (*Old Jew and a Boy*,

Spanish Woman from Mallorca, Girl on a Ball). These canvases are among the most significant works of Pablo Picasso; they are permeated with the artist's utmost compassion for man. The key theme of the early Picasso is that of friendship, sympathy for people and mutual support in a cheerless and cruel world. None of the avantgarde trends of the early twentieth century broke with the tradition so dramatically as Cubism. In his Cubist pieces (*Portrait of Ambroise Vollard, Queen Isabeau, Woman with a Fan* and *Still Life with a Violin*) Picasso totally rejected the world of material objects, eliminated bright colours and defined volumes with the help of broken, overlapping planes.

The seventeen Matisses displayed in the Museum date from various periods of the artist's career. Most of them were executed by Matisse between 1900 and 1920. They include such masterpieces as *Statuette and Vases on an Oriental Carpet, Still Life with Goldfish, The Painter's Studio, Nasturtiums and "The Dance"* and *Azure Vase with Flowers on a Blue Tablecloth*. Matisse's work is based on the harmony of brilliant and pure colours and on the musical rhythm of silhouettes. His pictures are imbued with the feeling of fullness of life, the beauty of the world and man.

Georges Rouault, Maurice Vlaminck and André Derain are represented by their early, mostly Fauvist, works. The landscapes by Albert Marquet are acknowledged as the finest achievements in this genre in twentieth-century French art. The Museum possesses a considerable number of works by French artists of the early twentieth century — Henri Rousseau, Maurice Denis, Pierre Bonnard and Jean Édouard Vuillard.

The subsequent period in the history of twentieth-century painting is represented in the Museum less systematically, although the part of the collection devoted to it boasts some outstanding works by the German artists Hans Grundig and Bert Heller, the Frenchmen

Amédée Ozenfant, Léopold Survage, Fernand Léger and Raoul Dufy, the Italians Giorgio de' Chirico, Achille Funi and Renato Guttuso, the Czechs Josef Čapek and Antonín Procházka, the Americans Rockwell Kent and Anton Refregier, the Mexicans Diego Rivera and David Alfaro Siqueiros, the Spaniards Joan Miró and Albert Sánchez, the Romanian Corneliu Baba, the Bulgarian Zlatu Bojadgiev.

Today the Pushkin Museum of Fine Arts, one of the best art museums in the Soviet Union, possesses an impressive collection of the Old Masters and an interesting and comprehensive collection of works by contemporary artists, which gives an ample idea of the diversity and peculiarity of trends in twentieth-century art.

PLATES

1. BYZANTINE MASTER
OF THE 14TH CENTURY
St. Pantaleon

2. BYZANTINE MASTER OF THE 14TH CENTURY
The Twelve Apostles. First half of the 14th century

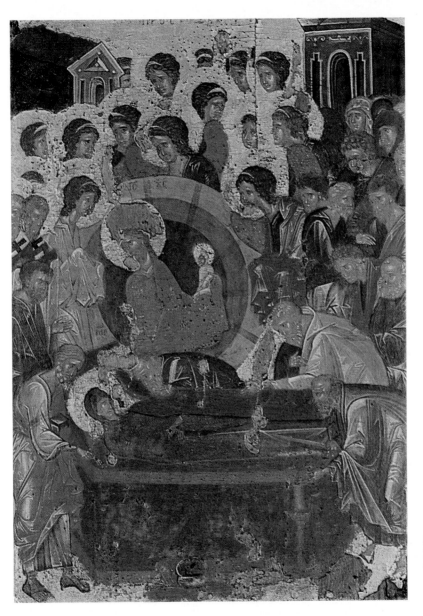

3. BYZANTINE
MASTER OF THE
14TH CENTURY
The Dormition.
First half of the
14th century

4. FLORENTINE MASTER OF THE SECOND HALF OF THE 13TH CENTURY
Madonna and Child Enthroned.
C. 1275—80

5. PISAN MASTER OF THE SECOND
HALF OF THE 13TH CENTURY
Madonna and Child Enthroned. *C.* 1280

6. FLORENTINE MASTER OF THE
SECOND HALF OF THE 14TH CENTURY
Madonna and Child with Saints.
The Nativity. The Crucifixion.
Triptych. Last quarter of the 14th century

7. FRANCESCO D'ANTONIO DE ANCONA.
Active in the second half of the 14th century
Madonna and Child with Saints. Polyptych. 1393

8. SASSETTA
(STEFANO
DI GIOVANNI).
C. 1392—1450
St. Lawrence.
St. Stephen. Panels
of polyptych. First
half of the 15th
century

9. SANO DI PIETRO. 1406—1481
The Beheading of John the Baptist

10. SANDRO BOTTICELLI
(ALESSANDRO DI
MARIANO DEI FILIPEPI).
1444/45—1510
The Annunciation. Parts
of an altarpiece. 1490s

11. PERUGINO (PIETRO VANNUCCI). *C.* 1450—1523
Madonna and Child. 1490s

12. GIOVANNI ANTONIO BOLTRAFFIO. 1466/67—1516
St. Sebastian. Late 15th century

13. PAOLO VERONESE
(PAOLO CALIARI). 1528—1588
Minerva. Sketch for a mural.
1560s

14. BRONZINO (AGNOLO DI COSIMO DI MARIANO). 1503—1572
The Holy Family and John the Baptist. 1530s

15. BERNARDO CAVALLINO. 1616—1656
Heliodorus Driven from the Temple

16. GIUSEPPE MARIA CRESPI. 1665—1747
Nymphs Disarming Cupids. 1690s

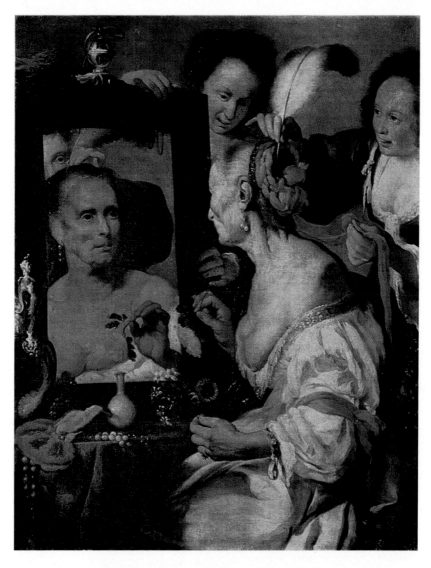

17. BERNARDO STROZZI (IL PRETE GENOVESE). 1581—1644
An Old Coquette. 1620s

18. GIOVANNI BATTISTA
TIEPOLO. 1696—1770
Two Saints. Sketch for an
altarpiece. 1740—45

19. GIOVANNI BATTISTA TIEPOLO. 1696—1770
The Death of Dido. Sketch. 1757—60

20. ALESSANDRO MAGNASCO. 1667—1749
Clown Training a Magpie

21. FRANCESCO GUARDI. 1712—1793
Alexander the Great Before the Corpse of Darius. 1740

22. FRANCESCO
GUARDI. 1712—1793
A View in Venice. 1770s

23. CANALETTO (GIOVANNI ANTONIO CANALE). 1697—1768
The Betrothal of the Venetian Doge to the Adriatic Sea. 1720s

24. PEDRO ESPALARGUES (?).
Active in the late 15th and
early 16th century
The Archangel Michael
Weighing Souls of the Dead.
First quarter of the 16th
century

25. FRANCISCO DE ZURBARÁN. 1598—1664
The Virgin and Child. 1658

26. JOSÉ DE RIBERA. 1591—1652
The Apostle James the Elder. 1647

27. BARTOLOMÉ ESTEBAN MURILLO. 1617—1682
Girl Selling Fruit. 1650s

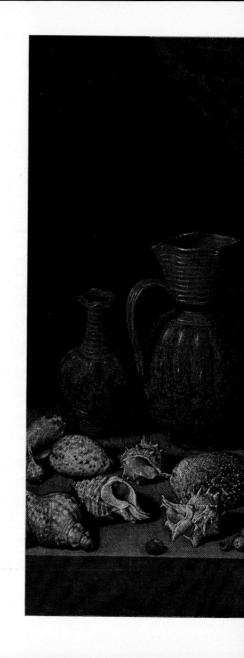

28. ANTONIO DE PEREDA. 1608—1678
Still Life with a Clock. 1652

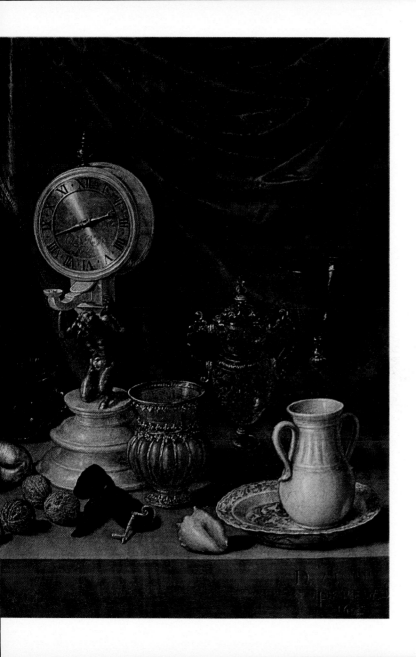

29. AUSTRIAN
MASTER OF THE
15TH CENTURY
Mary in a Dress
Patterned with Ears
of Corn. Meeting of
St. Joachim and St. Anne
Panels of an altarpiece.
Mid-15th century

30. MASTER OF THE
LIECHTENSTEIN CASTLE. Active in
the mid-15th century
The Nativity. Panel of the Sebenstein
altarpiece

31. JOHANN
 KOERBECKE. ? — 1491
The Flagellation.
C. 1457

32. LUCAS CRANACH
THE ELDER. 1472—1553
The Effects of Jealousy
(The Silver Age). 1530

33. LUCAS CRANACH
THE ELDER. 1472—1553
The Virgin and Child.
Fragment. *C.* 1525

34. MATTHIAS GERUNG.
C. 1500 — *c.* 1570
The Allegory of Love.
1530s

35. MASTER OF HOOGSTRAETEN.
Active in the early 16th century
The Annunciation. *C.* 1500—10

36. MICHIEL SITTOW. 1469—1525
Carrying the Cross. Early 16th century

37. HERRI MET DE BLES. *C.* 1510 — *c.* 1559
The Road to Calvary. *C.* 1540—50

38. JOACHIM BUECKELAER. *C.* 1530—1574
In the Market-place. 1564

39. JAN BRUEGHEL THE ELDER (VELVET BRUEGHEL). 1568—1625
Landscape. 1603

40. PETER PAUL RUBENS. 1577—1640
The Last Supper. *C.* 1630

41. PETER PAUL RUBENS. 1577—1640
Bacchanalia. *C.* 1615

42. ANTHONY VAN DYCK. 1599—1641
Portrait of Jan van den Wouwer. *C.* 1632

43. HENDRICK AVERCAMP. 1585—1634
Winter Scene with Skaters. *C.* 1630

44. JACOB JORDAENS. 1593—1678
Ulysses in the Cavern of Polyphemus. *C*. 1635

45. JAN VAN GOYEN. 1596—1656
View of the Waal at Nijmegen. 1649

46. JACOB ISAACKSZ. VAN RUISDAEL. 1628—1682
View of Egmond aan Zee. *C*. 1649

47. FRANS SNYDERS. 1579—1657
Still Life with a Swan. *C.* 1615—20

48. PIETER CLAESZ. *C.* 1597—1661
Still Life. 1646

49. WILLEM CLAESZ. HEDA. 1594—1680/82
Ham and Silverware. 1649

50. GABRIEL METSU. 1629—1667
Girl Doing Needlework. Late 1650s — early 1660s

51. ADRIAEN VAN OSTADE. 1610—1685
Drunken Brawl. *C.* 1635

52. ADRIAEN VAN OSTADE. 1610—1685
Flute Player. *C*. 1660

53. REMBRANDT HARMENSZ. VAN RIJN. 1606—1669
Ahasuerus, Haman and Esther. 1660

54. REMBRANDT HARMENSZ. VAN RIJN. 1606—1669
Christ Driving the Money-changers from the Temple. 1626

55. REMBRANDT HARMENSZ. VAN RIJN. 1606—1669
Portrait of an Old Woman. 1654

56. LEONAERT BRAMER. 1596—1674
David Dancing Before the Lord. *C.* 1630

57. EMANUEL DE WITTE. 1616/17—1692.
A Church Interior. 1670s

58. EMANUEL DE WITTE. 1616/17—1692
Market in the Port. 1660s

59. JAN VAN KESSEL. 1641/42—1680
Bleaching Linen. 1660s—1670s

60. PIETER DE HOOCH. 1629 — after 1684
A Sick Child. 1670s

61. GERARD TER BORCH. 1617—1681
Portrait of a Lady. 1660s

62. NICOLAS POUSSIN. 1594—1665
The Victory of Joshua over the Amorites. *C.* 1625

63. NICOLAS POUSSIN. 1594—1665
Rinaldo and Armida. 1630s

64. NICOLAS POUSSIN. 1594—1665
The Magnanimity of Scipio. 1640s

65. UNKNOWN FRENCH ARTIST.
Active in the second half of the 17th century
Portrait of a Horseman in Blue. 1670s

66. NICOLAS DE LARGILLIÈRE. 1656—1746
Portrait of a Young Lady. *C.* 1710

67. ANTOINE WATTEAU. 1684—1721
Satire on Physicians. *C.* 1708

68. CLAUDE GELLÉE (CLAUDE LORRAIN). 1600—1682
The Rape of Europa. 1655

69. NICOLAS LANCRET. 1690—1743
Portrait of a Lady in the Garden. 1730s

70. JEAN-BAPTISTE FRANÇOIS PATER. 1695—1736
The Maypole Festival. Early 1730s

71. CLAUDE JOSEPH VERNET. 1714—1789
View of the Park of Villa Pamphili. 1749

72. FRANÇOIS BOUCHER. 1703—1770
Jupiter and Callisto. 1744

73. EUGÈNE DELACROIX. 1798—1863
After the Shipwreck. *C.* 1847

74. JACQUES LOUIS DAVID. 1748—1825
Self-portrait. *C.* 1789

75. JEAN-BAPTISTE SIMÉON CHARDIN. 1699—1779
Still Life with the Attributes of the Arts. 1750s

76. THÉODORE GÉRICAULT. 1791—1824
Study of a Male Model. *C.* 1810—11

77. JOHN CONSTABLE. 1776—1837
View of Highgate from Hampstead Heath. *C.* 1835

78. CHARLES FRANÇOIS DAUBIGNY. 1817—1878
Evening in Honfleur. 1860s

79. CHARLES FRANÇOIS DAUBIGNY. 1817—1878
The Seashore. 1860s

80. JEAN-BAPTISTE CAMILLE COROT. 1796—1875
Stormy Weather. The Shore of Pas-de-Calais. *C*. 1870s

81. JEAN-BAPTISTE CAMILLE COROT. 1796—1875
Château de Pierrefonds. 1850s—1860s

82. JEAN-BAPTISTE CAMILLE COROT. 1796—1875
Haycart. 1860s

83. GUSTAVE COURBET. 1819—1877
A Hut in the Mountains. *C.* 1874

84. JULES DUPRÉ. 1811—1889
Oaks by the Road. 1830s

85. ÉDOUARD MANET. 1832—1883
Portrait of Antonin Proust. Before 1880

86. ÉDOUARD MANET. 1832—1883
In the Bar ("Le Bouchon"). 1878—79

87. EDGAR DEGAS. 1834—1917
Dancer at the Photographer's. Between 1874 and 1877

88. EDGAR DEGAS. 1834—1917
Exercising Race-horses. 1860s

89. CAMILLE PISSARRO. 1830—1903
Ploughland. 1874

90. ALFRED SISLEY. 1839—1899
Frosty Morning in Louveciennes. 1873

91. PIERRE AUGUSTE RENOIR. 1841—1919
Bathing on the Seine ("La Grenouillère"). 1869

92. PIERRE AUGUSTE RENOIR. 1841—1919
Portrait of the Actress Jeanne Samary. 1877

93. PIERRE AUGUSTE RENOIR. 1841—1919
Nude. 1876

94. CLAUDE MONET. 1840—1926
Luncheon on the Grass. 1866

95. CLAUDE MONET.
1840—1926
Rouen Cathedral at
Sunset. 1894

96. CLAUDE MONET.
1840—1926
Rouen Cathedral
at Noon. 1894

97. PAUL CÉZANNE. 1839—1906
Self-portrait. *C.* 1880

98. PAUL CÉZANNE. 1839—1906
Pierrot and Harlequin (Mardi Gras). 1888

99. PAUL CÉZANNE. 1839—1906
Landscape at Aix (Mount Sainte-Victoire). *C.* 1905

100. PAUL CÉZANNE. 1839—1906
Still Life with Peaches and Pears. 1888—90

101. PAUL GAUGUIN. 1848—1903
Gathering Fruit. 1899

102. PAUL GAUGUIN. 1848—1903
The King's Wife. 1896

103. PAUL GAUGUIN. 1848—1903
The Great Buddha. 1899

104. PAUL GAUGUIN. 1848—1903
Her Name Is Vaïraumati. 1892

105. VINCENT VAN GOGH. 1853—1890
The Convict Prison. 1890

106. VINCENT VAN GOGH. 1853—1890
The Red Vineyard at Arles. 1888

107. HENRI DE TOULOUSE-LAUTREC. 1864—1901
The Singer Yvette Guilbert. 1894

108. ÉDOUARD VUILLARD. 1868—1940
In the Garden. *C*. 1894—95

109. PIERRE BONNARD. 1867—1947
Mirror Above the Washstand. *C.* 1908

110. PIERRE BONNARD. 1867—1947
Summer in Normandy. *C*. 1911—12

111. HENRI ROUSSEAU. 1844—1910
The Poet and His Muse. Portrait of Apollinaire and Marie Laurencin. 1909

112. MAURICE UTRILLO. 1883—1955
A White House (In a Poor District). *C.* 1912

113. PABLO PICASSO. 1881—1973
The Strolling Acrobats. 1901

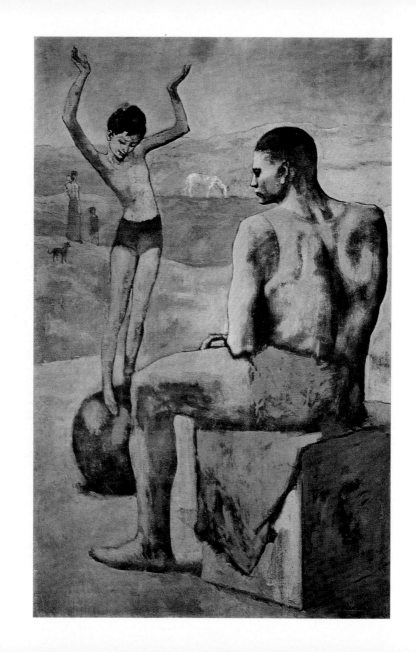

114. PABLO PICASSO.
1881—1973
Girl on a Ball. 1905

115. PABLO PICASSO. 1881—1973
Old Jew and a Boy. 1903

116. PABLO PICASSO. 1881—1973
Portrait of Ambroise Vollard. 1909—10

117. MAURICE VLAMINCK. 1876—1958
River. *C.* 1912

118. PAUL SIGNAC. 1863—1935
The Pine-tree. Saint-Tropez. 1909

119. RAOUL DUFY. 1877—1953
July 14 in Deauville. 1933

120. GEORGES BRAQUE. 1882—1963
The New Castle at La Roche-Guyon. 1909

121. ALBERT MARQUET. 1875—1947
Mount Vesuvius. 1909

122. ALBERT MARQUET. 1875—1947
Harbour at Honfleur. 1911

123. HENRI MATISSE.
1869—1954
Still Life with
Goldfish. 1911

124. HENRI MATISSE. 1869—1954
The Painter's Studio. 1911

125. HENRI MATISSE. 1869—1954
Statuette and Vases on an Oriental Carpet. 1908

126. ANDRÉ DERAIN. 1880—1954
Fishing Boats (Drying Sails). 1905

127. ANDRÉ DERAIN. 1880—1954
Saturday. Between 1911 and 1914

128. FERNAND LÉGER. 1881—1955
Composition. 1918

129. FERNAND LÉGER. 1881—1955
Builders with Aloe. 1951

130. MAX LIEBERMANN. 1847—1935
Young Girl with a Cow. *C.* 1885—90

131. ANDERS ZORN. 1860—1920
Portrait of Savva Mamontov, 1896

132. EDVARD MUNCH. 1863—1944
White Night (Girls on the Bridge). 1903

133. RENATO GUTTUSO. 1912—1987
Calabrian Worker's Sunday in Rome (Rocco with a Gramophone). 1960—61

134. GIORGIO DE'CHIRICO. 1888—1978
Women of Rome. 1926

135. ACHILLE FUNI. 1890—1972
Rebecca at the Well. 1924

136. MARY CASSATT. 1845—1926
Mother and Child. 1890s

137. ROCKWELL KENT. 1882—1971
Eskimo in a Kayak. 1933

LIST OF PLATES

1. BYZANTINE MASTER OF THE
14TH CENTURY
St. Pantaleon
Tempera on panel. 53×34 cm

2. BYZANTINE MASTER OF THE
14TH CENTURY
Constantinople school
The Twelve Apostles. First half of
the 14th century
Tempera on panel. 38×34 cm

3. BYZANTINE MASTER OF THE
14TH CENTURY
Constantinople school
The Dormition. First half of the
14th century
Tempera on panel. 45×34 cm

4. FLORENTINE MASTER OF THE
SECOND HALF OF THE 13TH
CENTURY
Italian school
Madonna and Child Enthroned.
C. 1275—80
Tempera on panel. 246×138 cm

5. PISAN MASTER OF THE SECOND
HALF OF THE 13TH CENTURY
Italian school
Madonna and Child Enthroned.
C. 1280
Tempera on panel. 173×84 cm

6. FLORENTINE MASTER OF THE
SECOND HALF OF THE 14TH
CENTURY
Italian school
Madonna and Child with Saints.
The Nativity. The Crucifixion.
Triptych. Last quarter of the
14th century
Tempera on panel. 75×56 cm

7. FRANCESCO D'ANTONIO DE
ANCONA. Active in the second half
of the 14th century
Italian school
Madonna and Child with Saints.
Polyptych. 1393
Tempera on panel. 195×235 cm

8. SASSETTA (STEFANO DI
GIOVANNI). C. 1392—1450
Italian school
St. Lawrence. St. Stephen. Panels
of polyptych. First half of the
15th century
Tempera on panel. 76×25 cm
(each panel)

9. SANO DI PIETRO. 1406—1481
Italian school
The Beheading of John the Baptist
Tempera on panel. 24×34 cm

10. SANDRO BOTTICELLI
(ALESSANDRO DI MARIANO DEI
FILIPEPI). 1444/45—1510
Italian school
The Annunciation. Parts of an
altarpiece. 1490s
Tempera on canvas (transferred
from panel). 45×13 cm
(each part)

11. PERUGINO (PIETRO
VANNUCCI). C. 1450—1523
Italian school
Madonna and Child. 1490s
Oil on canvas (transferred from
panel). 51×38 cm

12. GIOVANNI ANTONIO
BOLTRAFFIO. 1466/67—1516
Italian school

St. Sebastian. Late 15th century
Oil on canvas (transferred from panel). 48×36 cm

13. PAOLO VERONESE (PAOLO CALIARI). 1528—1588
Italian school
Minerva. Sketch for a mural. 1560s
Oil on canvas. 28×16 cm

14. BRONZINO (AGNOLO DI COSIMO DI MARIANO). 1503—1572
Italian school
The Holy Family and John the Baptist. 1530s
Oil on canvas
(transferred from panel).
117×99 cm

15. BERNARDO CAVALLINO.
1616—1656
Italian school
Heliodorus Driven from the Temple
Oil on copper plate. 62×88 cm

16. GIUSEPPE MARIA CRESPI.
1665—1747
Italian school
Nymphs Disarming Cupids. 1690s
Oil on copper plate. 52×74 cm

17. BERNARDO STROZZI (IL PRETE GENOVESE). 1581—1644
Italian school
An Old Coquette. 1620s
Oil on canvas. 135×109 cm

18. GIOVANNI BATTISTA TIEPOLO.
1696—1770
Italian school
Two Saints. Sketch for an altarpiece. 1740—45
Oil on canvas. 61×36 cm

19. GIOVANNI BATTISTA TIEPOLO.
1696—1770
Italian school
The Death of Dido. Sketch. 1757—60
Oil on canvas. 40×63 cm

20. ALESSANDRO MAGNASCO.
1667—1749
Italian school
Clown Training a Magpie
Oil on canvas. 40×31 cm

21. FRANCESCO GUARDI. 1712—1793
Italian school
Alexander the Great Before the Corpse of Darius. 1740
Oil on canvas. 95×126 cm

22. FRANCESCO GUARDI. 1712—1793
Italian school
A View in Venice. 1770s
Oil on canvas. 38×26 cm

23. CANALETTO (GIOVANNI ANTONIO CANALE). 1697—1768
Italian school
The Betrothal of the Venetian Doge to the Adriatic Sea. 1720s
Oil on canvas. 182×259 cm

24. PEDRO ESPALARGUES (?).
Active in the late 15th and early 16th century
Spanish school
The Archangel Michael Weighing Souls of the Dead. First quarter of the 16th century
Tempera on panel. 172×90 cm

25. FRANCISCO DE ZURBARÁN.
1598—1664
Spanish school
The Virgin and Child. 1658
Oil on canvas. 101×78 cm

26. JOSÉ DE RIBERA. 1591—1652
Spanish school
The Apostle James the Elder. 1647
Oil on canvas. 92×72 cm

27. BARTOLOMÉ ESTEBAN
MURILLO. 1617—1682
Spanish school
Girl Selling Fruit. 1650s
Oil on canvas. 76×61 cm

28. ANTONIO DE PEREDA. 1608—1678
Spanish school
Still Life with a Clock. 1652
Oil on canvas. 78×91 cm

29. AUSTRIAN MASTER OF THE
15TH CENTURY
Mary in a Dress Patterned with
Ears of Corn. Meeting of
St. Joachim and St. Anne. Panels
of an altarpiece. Mid-15th century
Tempera on panel. 124×40 cm

30. MASTER OF THE LIECHTENSTEIN
CASTLE. Active in the mid-15th
century
Austrian school
The Nativity. Panel of the
Sebenstein altarpiece
Oil on panel. 101×50 cm

31. JOHANN KOERBECKE. ?—1491
German school
The Flagellation. C. 1457
Tempera on panel. 93×65 cm

32. LUCAS CRANACH THE ELDER.
1472—1553
German school
The Effects of Jealousy (The
Silver Age). 1530
Oil on panel. 56.5×48.5 cm

33. LUCAS CRANACH THE ELDER.
1472—1553
German school
The Virgin and Child. Fragment.
C. 1525
Oil on panel. 58×46 cm

34. MATTHIAS GERUNG. C. 1500 —
c. 1570
German school
The Allegory of Love. 1530s
Oil on panel. 51×33 cm

35. MASTER OF HOOGSTRAETEN.
Active in the early 16th century
Netherlandish school
The Annunciation. C. 1500—10
Oil on panel. 34×25 cm

36. MICHIEL SITTOW. 1469—1525
Netherlandish school
Carrying the Cross. Early 16th
century
Oil on panel. 37×29 cm

37. HERRI MET DE BLES. C. 1510 —
c. 1559
Netherlandish school
The Road to Calvary. C. 1540—50
Oil on panel. 39×50 cm

38. JOACHIM BUECKELAER.
C. 1530—1574
Netherlandish school
In the Market-place. 1564
Oil on panel. 128×166 cm

39. JAN BRUEGHEL THE ELDER
(VELVET BRUEGHEL). 1568—1625
Flemish school
Landscape. 1603
Oil on copper plate. 17.8×24.5 cm

40. PETER PAUL RUBENS.
1577—1640
Flemish school
The Last Supper. *C.* 1630
Oil on panel. 46×41 cm

41. PETER PAUL RUBENS.
1577—1640
Flemish school
Bacchanalia. *C.* 1615
Oil on canvas (transferred from panel). 91×107 cm

42. ANTHONY VAN DYCK. 1599—1641
Flemish school
Portrait of Jan van den Wouwer.
C. 1632
Oil on canvas (transferred from panel). 106×86 cm

43. HENDRICK AVERCAMP. 1585—1634
Dutch school
Winter Scene with Skaters. *C.* 1630
Oil on panel. 24×38 cm

44. JACOB JORDAENS. 1593—1678
Flemish school
Ulysses in the Cavern
of Polyphemus. *C.* 1635
Oil on canvas mounted on panel.
76×96 cm

45. JAN VAN GOYEN. 1596—1656
Dutch school
View of the Waal at Nijmegen. 1649
Oil on panel. 39×62 cm

46. JACOB ISAACKSZ. VAN
RUISDAEL. 1628—1682
Dutch school
View of Egmond aan Zee. *C.* 1649
Oil on panel. 45×37 cm

47. FRANS SNYDERS. 1579—1657
Flemish school
Still Life with a Swan. *C.* 1615—20
Oil on canvas. 162.5×235 cm

48. PIETER CLAESZ. *C.* 1597—1661
Dutch school
Still Life. 1646
Oil on panel. 60×84 cm

49. WILLEM CLAESZ. HEDA.
1594—1680/82
Dutch school
Ham and Silverware. 1649
Oil on panel. 97×80.5 cm

50. GABRIEL METSU. 1629—1667
Dutch school
Girl Doing Needlework.
Late 1650s — early 1660s
Oil on panel. 35×27 cm

51. ADRIAEN VAN OSTADE.
1610—1685
Dutch school
Drunken Brawl. *C.* 1635
Oil on panel. 41×55 cm

52. ADRIAEN VAN OSTADE. 1610—1685
Dutch school
Flute Player. *C.* 1660
Oil on panel. 29×23 cm

53. REMBRANDT HARMENSZ. VAN
RIJN. 1606—1669
Dutch school
Ahasuerus, Haman and Esther. 1660
Oil on canvas. 73×94 cm

54. REMBRANDT HARMENSZ. VAN
RIJN. 1606—1669
Dutch school

Christ Driving the Money-changers
from the Temple. 1626
Oil on panel. 43×33 cm

55. REMBRANDT HARMENSZ. VAN
RIJN. 1606—1669
Dutch school
Portrait of an Old Woman. 1654
Oil on canvas. 74×63 cm

56. LEONAERT BRAMER. 1596—1674
Dutch school
David Dancing Before the Lord.
C. 1630
Oil on copper plate. 42×58 cm

57. EMANUEL DE WITTE.
1616/17—1692
Dutch school
A Church Interior. 1670s
Oil on panel. 68×51 cm

58. EMANUEL DE WITTE.
1616/17—1692
Dutch school
Market in the Port. 1660s
Oil on canvas. 60.7×75.5 cm

59. JAN VAN KESSEL. 1641/42—1680
Dutch school
Bleaching Linen. 1660s—1670s
Oil on canvas. 55.5×67.5 cm

60. PIETER DE HOOCH. 1629 —
after 1684
Dutch school
A Sick Child. 1670s
Oil on canvas. 52×61 cm

61. GERARD TER BORCH. 1617—1681
Dutch school
Portrait of a Lady. 1660s
Oil on canvas. 62×46 cm

62. NICOLAS POUSSIN. 1594—1665
French school
The Victory of Joshua over the
Amorites. C. 1625
Oil on canvas. 96×130 cm

63. NICOLAS POUSSIN. 1594—1665
French school
Rinaldo and Armida. 1630s
Oil on canvas. 95×133 cm

64. NICOLAS POUSSIN. 1594—1665
French school
The Magnanimity of Scipio. 1640s
Oil on canvas. 114.5×163.5 cm

65. UNKNOWN FRENCH ARTIST.
Active in the second half of the
17th century
Portrait of a Horseman in Blue.
1670s
Oil on canvas. 46×35 cm

66. NICOLAS DE LARGILLIÈRE.
1656—1746
French school
Portrait of a Young Lady.
C. 1710
Oil on canvas. 80×64 cm (oval)

67. ANTOINE WATTEAU. 1684—1721
French school
Satire on Physicians. C. 1708
Oil on panel. 26×37 cm

68. CLAUDE GELLÉE (CLAUDE
LORRAIN). 1600—1682
French school
The Rape of Europa. 1655
Oil on canvas. 100×137 cm

69. NICOLAS LANCRET. 1690—1743
French school

Portrait of a Lady in the Garden.
1730s
Oil on canvas. 37×47 cm

70. JEAN-BAPTISTE FRANÇOIS
PATER. 1695—1736
French school
The Maypole Festival. Early 1730s
Oil on canvas. 34×44 cm

71. CLAUDE JOSEPH VERNET.
1714—1789
French school
View of the Park of Villa
Pamphili. 1749
Oil on canvas. 76×101 cm

72. FRANÇOIS BOUCHER. 1703—1770
French school
Jupiter and Callisto. 1744
Oil on canvas. 98×72 cm

73. EUGÈNE DELACROIX. 1798—1863
French school
After the Shipwreck. C. 1847
Oil on canvas. 36×57 cm

74. JACQUES LOUIS DAVID.
1748—1825
French school
Self-portrait. C. 1789
Oil on canvas. 63×52 cm

75. JEAN-BAPTISTE SIMÉON
CHARDIN. 1699—1779
French school
Still Life with the Attributes of
the Arts. 1750s
Oil on canvas. 53×110 cm

76. THÉODORE GÉRICAULT.
1791—1824
French school

Study of a Male Model.
C. 1810—11
Oil on canvas. 64×53 cm

77. JOHN CONSTABLE. 1776—1837
English school
View of Highgate from Hampstead
Heath. C. 1835
Oil on cardboard. 24×29.5 cm

78. CHARLES FRANÇOIS DAUBIGNY.
1817—1878
French school
Evening in Honfleur. 1860s
Oil on panel. 19×34 cm

79. CHARLES FRANÇOIS DAUBIGNY.
1817—1878
French school
The Seashore. 1860s
Oil on panel. 20×34 cm

80. JEAN-BAPTISTE CAMILLE COROT.
1796—1875
French school
Stormy Weather. The Shore of
Pas-de-Calais. C. 1870s
Oil on canvas. 39×55 cm

81. JEAN-BAPTISTE CAMILLE COROT.
1796—1875
French school
Château de Pierrefonds.
1850s—1860s
Oil on panel. 47×38 cm

82. JEAN-BAPTISTE CAMILLE COROT.
1796—1875
French school
Haycart. 1860s
Oil on canvas. 32×45 cm

83. GUSTAVE COURBET. 1819—1877
French school
A Hut in the Mountains. *C.* 1874
Oil on canvas. 33×49 cm

84. JULES DUPRÉ. 1811—1889
French school
Oaks by the Road. 1830s
Oil on canvas. 43×58 cm

85. ÉDOUARD MANET. 1832—1883
French school
Portrait of Antonin Proust.
Before 1880
Oil on canvas. 65×54 cm

86. ÉDOUARD MANET. 1832—1883
French school
In the Bar ("Le Bouchon").
1878—79
Oil on canvas. 72×92 cm

87. EDGAR DEGAS. 1834—1917
French school
Dancer at the Photographer's.
Between 1874 and 1877
Oil on canvas. 65×50 cm

88. EDGAR DEGAS. 1834—1917
French school
Exercising Race-horses. 1860s
Pastel on paper. 36×86 cm

89. CAMILLE PISSARRO. 1830—1903
French school
Ploughland. 1874
Oil on canvas. 49×64 cm

90. ALFRED SISLEY. 1839—1899
French school
Frosty Morning in Louveciennes.
1873
Oil on canvas. 46×61 cm

91. PIERRE AUGUSTE RENOIR.
1841—1919
French school
Bathing on the Seine
("La Grenouillère"). 1869
Oil on canvas. 59×80 cm

92. PIERRE AUGUSTE RENOIR.
1841—1919
French school
Portrait of the Actress Jeanne
Samary. 1877
Oil on canvas. 56×47 cm

93. PIERRE AUGUSTE RENOIR.
1841—1919
French school
Nude. 1876
Oil on canvas. 92×73 cm

94. CLAUDE MONET. 1840—1926
French school
Luncheon on the Grass. 1866
Oil on canvas. 130×181 cm

95. CLAUDE MONET. 1840—1926
French school
Rouen Cathedral at Sunset. 1894
Oil on canvas. 101×65 cm

96. CLAUDE MONET. 1840—1926
French school
Rouen Cathedral at Noon. 1894
Oil on canvas. 100×65 cm

97. PAUL CÉZANNE. 1839—1906
French school
Self-portrait. *C.* 1880
Oil on canvas. 45×37 cm

98. PAUL CÉZANNE. 1839—1906
French school

Pierrot and Harlequin (Mardi Gras). 1888
Oil on canvas. 102×81 cm

99. PAUL CÉZANNE. 1839—1906
French school
Landscape at Aix (Mount Sainte-Victoire). *C.* 1905
Oil on canvas. 60×73 cm

100. PAUL CÉZANNE. 1839—1906
French school
Still Life with Peaches and Pears. 1888—90
Oil on canvas. 61×90 cm

101. PAUL GAUGUIN. 1848—1903
French school
Gathering Fruit. 1899
Oil on canvas. 130×190 cm

102. PAUL GAUGUIN. 1848—1903
French school
The King's Wife. 1896
Oil on canvas. 97×130 cm

103. PAUL GAUGUIN. 1848—1903
French school
The Great Buddha. 1899
Oil on canvas. 134×95 cm

104. PAUL GAUGUIN. 1848—1903
French school
Her Name Is Vaïraumati. 1892
Oil on canvas. 91×68 cm

105. VINCENT VAN GOGH. 1853—1890
Dutch school
The Convict Prison. 1890
Oil on canvas. 80×64 cm

106. VINCENT VAN GOGH. 1853—1890
Dutch school

The Red Vineyard at Arles. 1888
Oil on canvas. 73×91 cm

107. HENRI DE TOULOUSE-LAUTREC. 1864—1901
French school
The Singer Yvette Guilbert. 1894
Tempera and oil on cardboard. 57×42 cm

108. ÉDOUARD VUILLARD. 1868—1940
French school
In the Garden. *C.* 1894—95
Tempera on cardboard. 51×83 cm

109. PIERRE BONNARD. 1867—1947
French school
Mirror Above the Washstand. *C.* 1908
Oil on canvas. 120×97 cm

110. PIERRE BONNARD. 1867—1947
French school
Summer in Normandy. *C.* 1911—12
Oil on canvas. 114×128 cm

111. HENRI ROUSSEAU. 1844—1910
French school
The Poet and His Muse.
Portrait of Apollinaire and Marie Laurencin. 1909
Oil on canvas. 131×97 cm

112. MAURICE UTRILLO. 1883—1955
French school
A White House (In a Poor District). *C.* 1912
Oil on canvas. 65×81 cm

113. PABLO PICASSO. 1881—1973
Spanish school
The Strolling Acrobats. 1901
Oil on canvas. 73×60 cm

114. PABLO PICASSO. 1881—1973
Spanish school
Girl on a Ball. 1905
Oil on canvas. 147×95 cm

115. PABLO PICASSO. 1881—1973
Spanish school
Old Jew and a Boy. 1903
Oil on canvas. 125×92 cm

116. PABLO PICASSO. 1881—1973
Spanish school
Portrait of Ambroise Vollard.
1909—10
Oil on canvas. 93×66 cm

117. MAURICE VLAMINCK. 1876—1958
French school
River. C. 1912
Oil on canvas. 83×102 cm

118. PAUL SIGNAC. 1863—1935
French school
The Pine-tree. Saint-Tropez. 1909
Oil on canvas. 72×92 cm

119. RAOUL DUFY. 1877—1953
French school
July 14 in Deauville. 1933
Oil on canvas. 38×92 cm

120. GEORGES BRAQUE. 1882—1963
French school
The New Castle at La Roche-Guyon.
1909
Oil on canvas. 92×73 cm

121. ALBERT MARQUET. 1875—1947
French school
Mount Vesuvius. 1909
Oil on canvas. 61×80 cm

122. ALBERT MARQUET. 1875—1947
French school
Harbour at Honfleur. 1911
Oil on canvas. 65×81 cm

123. HENRI MATISSE. 1869—1954
French school
Still Life with Goldfish. 1911
Oil on canvas. 146×97 cm

124. HENRI MATISSE. 1869—1954
French school
The Painter's Studio. 1911
Oil on canvas. 179.5×221.3 cm

125. HENRI MATISSE. 1869—1954
French school
Statuette and Vases on an Oriental
Carpet. 1908
Oil on canvas. 88.5×105 cm

126. ANDRÉ DERAIN. 1880—1954
French school
Fishing Boats (Drying Sails). 1905
Oil on canvas. 82×101 cm

127. ANDRÉ DERAIN. 1880—1954
French school
Saturday. Between 1911 and 1914
Oil on canvas. 181×228 cm

128. FERNAND LÉGER. 1881—1955
French school
Composition. 1918
Oil on canvas. 146×114 cm

129. FERNAND LÉGER. 1881—1955
French school
Builders with Aloe. 1951
Oil on canvas. 160×200 cm

130. MAX LIEBERMANN. 1847—1935
German school

Young Girl with a Cow. *C.* 1885—90
Pastel on paper. 55×74 cm

131. ANDERS ZORN. 1860—1920
Swedish school
Portrait of Savva Mamontov. 1896
Oil on canvas. 130×97 cm

132. EDVARD MUNCH. 1863—1944
Norwegian school
White Night (Girls on the Bridge).
1903
Oil on canvas. 83×73 cm

133. RENATO GUTTUSO. 1912—1987
Italian school
Calabrian Worker's Sunday in Rome
(Rocco with a Gramophone).
1960—61
Oil on canvas. 188×152 cm

134. GIORGIO DE'CHIRICO. 1888—1978
Italian school
Women of Rome. 1926
Oil on canvas. 116×89 cm

135. ACHILLE FUNI. 1890—1972
Italian school
Rebecca at the Well. 1924
Oil on plywood. 97×86 cm

136. MARY CASSATT. 1845—1926
American school
Mother and Child. 1890s
Pastel on paper. 80×64 cm

137. ROCKWELL KENT. 1882—1971
American school
Eskimo in a Kayak. 1933
Oil on canvas. 82×87 cm

Государственный музей изобразительных искусств

имени А. С. Пушкина, Москва.

Живопись

Альбом (на английском языке)

Издание 2-е

Автор-составитель Ирина Александровна Антонова

Перевод с русского Е. Бессмертной

Художник Л. Зыков

Редактор В. Гусева

Редактор английского текста
Е. Табанюхина

Художественный редактор В. Матецкий

Технические редакторы Н. Голубева,
В. Иванова

Корректор Ю. Редькина

ИБ № 2326. Сдано в набор 20.11.86. Подписано в печать 17.12.87. Формат 70×75^1/$_{16}$. Бумага мелованная. Гарнитура обыкновенная. Высокая печать. Усл. печ л. 11,16. Усл. кр.-отт. 56,38. Уч.-изд. л. 9,37. Тираж 39 900. Заказ Т2460. Изд. № 1568. Цена 4 руб. Издательство ,,Аврора``. 191065, Ленинград, Невский пр., 7/9. Ленинградская типография № 3 Головное предприятие дважды ордена Трудового Красного Знамени Ленинградского производственного объединения ,,Типография имени Ивана Федорова`` Союзполиграфпрома при Государственном комитете СССР по делам издательств, полиграфии и книжной торговли. 191126, Ленинград, Звенигородская ул., 11